**Sports Illustrated KIDS**

# FOOTBALL'S GREATEST

## HAIL MARY PASSES
## AND OTHER CRUNCH-TIME HEROICS

BY MATT CHANDLER

T0052470

CAPSTONE PRESS
a capstone imprint

Captivate is published by Capstone Press, an imprint of Capstone.
1710 Roe Crest Drive, North Mankato, Minnesota 56003
www.capstonepub.com

**Library of Congress Cataloging-in-Publication Data is available on the Library of Congress website.**
ISBN 978-1-4966-8731-9 (hardcover)
ISBN 978-1-4966-8738-8 (paperback)
ISBN 978-1-4966-8739-5 (ebook PDF)

Summary: When time is running short and a big game is at stake, some players seize the moment and make themselves legends. From Hail Mary passes to tackle-breaking touchdown runs, some of football's greatest moments are replayed vividly here. You've got a sideline pass to the action.

**Photo Credits**
AP Photo: Tom Olmscheid, 23; Getty Images: Bettmann, 29, Leon Halip, 7, Stringer/Patrick Smith, 11, Stringer/Rick Stewart, 31; Newscom: KRT/Tom Lynn, 15, MCT/Charles Trainor Jr., 35, MCT/Lloyd Fox, 17, Reuters/Allen Fredrickson, 44 (bottom), Reuters/Rick Wilking, 13, Reuters/STR, 19, UPI/Brian Kersey, 9, UPI/Nell Redmond, 33, UPI Photo Service/Mike McCready, 25, USA Today Sports/Tim Fuller, 5; Shutterstock: Beto Chagas, cover (player), EFKS, cover (stadium), 1, silvae, cover (lights), 1; Sports Illustrated: Bob Rosato, 41, Damian Strohmeyer, 44 (top), Heinz Kluetmeier, 37, Neil Leifer, 26, 43, Peter Read Miller, 38, 39, Robert Beck, 21

**Editorial Credits**
Bobbie Nuytten, designer; Eric Gohl, media researcher; Katy LaVigne, production specialist

All internet sites appearing in back matter were available and accurate when this book was sent to press.

# TABLE OF CONTENTS

Words in **bold** are in the glossary.

# GAME-ENDING GREATNESS

Football is filled with great comebacks. They are part of what makes the game so exciting to watch. A team can be losing with one second left and throw a game-winning **Hail Mary** pass. A team can be 40 yards from the end zone but drill a clutch field goal as the clock runs out.

Teams have won games in many different ways. There have been passes and runs both short and long. There have been 100-yard kick returns. There have been broken tackles and tipped passes. And then there are the trick plays. Every team has a few plays ready for a last-second miracle. How can a coach steal a win? Maybe a flea flicker? A fake field goal? A halfback pass?

Does your favorite team have any memorable last-second wins? Read on to find out.

Aaron Rodgers leads the Packers in celebration after he completed a Hail Mary pass to defeat the Detroit Lions.

# CHAPTER 1

# HAIL MARY HEROES

## RODGERS TO RODGERS

The Green Bay Packers were in Detroit to take on the Lions in 2015. The Lions held a two-point lead, 23–21. The Packers had the ball but were 61 yards from the end zone with time for just one more play. Could Packers quarterback Aaron Rodgers make some magic?

The Packers lined up. Rodgers took the snap. Five Packers receivers took off. The Lions defense broke through. They chased Rodgers from the pocket. He scrambled to his right. From his own 35-yard line, Rodgers unloaded a long, high pass. The ball came down in the middle of a crowd of five Packers and five Lions in the end zone. Another Rodgers, Packers tight end Richard Rodgers, leaped high from the crowd. He pulled in the catch as he fell to the ground. The Packers had stunned the Lions with a miracle win in Detroit.

Packers tight end Richard Rodgers makes a catch amid a crowd of Lions defenders.

Aaron Rodgers and Richard Rodgers are not related. But they were both born in California. And they both played for the Cal Golden Bears in college.

# THE MINNESOTA MIRACLE

The Minnesota Vikings trailed the New Orleans Saints, 24–23, in a 2018 playoff game. The game was almost over. The Vikings were nearly beat. But a bit of time still remained.

With 25 seconds left, the Saints kicked a clutch field goal. It gave them the lead. The Vikings got the ball back. After two plays, they were at their own 39-yard line. The clock showed 10 seconds left in the game. The Vikings had no time-outs left.

Quarterback Case Keenum dropped back to pass. He threw a 25-yard pass toward Stefon Diggs. The speedy receiver leaped high. He caught the pass near the sideline with four seconds on the clock. If Diggs darted out of bounds, he could give his team one more chance. If the Saints tackled him in bounds, the clock would run out. Saints defender Marcus Williams rushed in to make the game-ending tackle. The defender dove at Diggs' legs . . . and missed!

Suddenly Diggs had a wide-open field. Diggs raced down the sideline for the 61-yard game-winning touchdown as the Minnesota home crowd roared in joyful surprise. The Minneapolis Miracle was a moment to remember.

Stefon Diggs dashed for a game-winning touchdown after making a leaping catch in the final seconds.

# TIP, TIP TOUCHDOWN

The Baltimore Ravens have long been known for their defense. So coming back from a 17–0 deficit against the Ravens would be tough. That is what Andy Dalton and the Cincinnati Bengals faced in a 2013 game. Slowly, the Bengals fought back. They scored 10 points in the second half. But time was running out. It looked like the comeback was going to fall short.

The Bengals faced fourth-and-fifteen from about midfield. Needing a touchdown, the Bengals went for the Hail Mary. Dalton launched the ball toward the end zone. The ball bounced off a crowd of players. It wobbled toward Ravens safety James Ihedigbo. All he had to do was let the ball fall to the ground and the Ravens would win. Instead, Ihedigbo tipped the ball. The ball sprang up into the air. Bengals receiver A.J. Green was standing alone in the back of the end zone. Green made an easy catch, stunning the Ravens home crowd.

Luckily for Raven fans, the Ravens pulled out the win in overtime with a field goal.

Ravens defenders were helpless as A.J. Green jumped to catch a Hail Mary pass.

## MR. CLUTCH

Peyton Manning led 54 game-winning drives in his career. One of his biggest came in 2003. Manning's Indianapolis Colts were battling the Tampa Bay Buccaneers. With less than four minutes left, the Bucs held a 35–14 lead. Then the Manning Magic kicked in. He led the Colts to 21 points to tie the game. In overtime, he finished the miracle when the Colts won 38–35 on a **sudden-death** field goal.

# DOUBLE CLUTCH

The only thing better than a clutch, last-second play is two in the same game. The Ravens trailed the host Denver Broncos 35–28 with 43 seconds to play in the 2012 American Football Conference (AFC) playoff game. With the ball at their own 30-yard line and time expiring, the Ravens were in trouble.

Then Joe Flacco showed off his incredible arm strength. The Ravens QB launched a pass deep down the right sideline. Ravens receiver Jacoby Jones beat the coverage and caught the 70-yard touchdown. Overtime!

The Broncos' stadium is 5,280 feet above sea level. The air is so thin that balls meet less resistance and can travel farther. This affects long-distance field goal attempts.

Both defenses played tough in overtime. With the game still tied at 35, the game went into double overtime. Playoff games, of course, cannot end in a tie.

It took Flacco and company only a few plays in the second overtime to make their move. Finally, Ravens kicker Justin Tucker drilled a 47-yard kick. The Ravens had the win.

Jacoby Jones prepares to nab a deep pass from Joe Flacco.

# CHAPTER 2

# PICK-SIX GEMS

## PACKERS PICK

It takes a lot of confidence to be a successful pro football player. In the 2003 National Football Conference (NFC) wildcard game, Seattle Seahawks quarterback Matt Hasselbeck had plenty of confidence. With the game tied at 27, the QB stood at midfield for the overtime coin toss. Hasselbeck won the toss. Referee Bernie Kukar asked if he wanted to receive the kick. Hasselbeck gave the most confident answer possible.

"We want the ball, and we're gonna score," he said. The quote was picked up on the referee's microphone. It was broadcast to more than 70,000 people, mostly Packers fans, at Lambeau Field in Green Bay. If Green Bay needed more motivation, Hasselbeck provided it.

Hasselbeck's opponent in the game was Brett Favre. He is the all-time leader in pick-six interceptions. He threw 35 during his 20-year National Football League (NFL) career.

Four minutes into overtime, the Packers made Hasselbeck pay. He threw a quick out pattern to wide receiver Alex Bannister. Packers cornerback Al Harris jumped the route for an easy interception. As Hasselbeck gave chase, Harris raced 56 yards for the **pick-six**. Harris scored a game-winning touchdown.

Defensive back Al Harris heads for the end zone after intercepting a pass in overtime.

# HEARTBREAKING PICK-SIX

When the Houston Texans hosted the Baltimore Ravens in 2010, Texans quarterback Matt Schaub had a big game. He threw for nearly 400 yards and three touchdowns. With the game tied at 28 at the end of regulation, he wasn't finished.

The Ravens won the coin toss. They got the ball first. The Texans' defense held strong. They forced a punt. Ravens punter Sam Koch pinned the Texans deep in their own end. Two plays later, disaster struck for Schaub and the Texans.

Schaub was under pressure in his own end zone. He was about to get sacked. Giving up a safety would have ended the game. Schaub tried to throw the ball away to avoid the sack. Ravens defensive back Josh Wilson was right there. He easily snagged the pass. He ran untouched into the end zone. Game over.

Schaub had played great football for four quarters. In an instant, his night was ruined, and the game was lost.

Texans QB Matt Schaub (left) mourns as
Josh Wilson celebrates a pick-six touchdown.

# PUNTER PROBLEMS

James Allen was in the right place at the right time for a bizarre pick-six. Allen's New Orleans Saints were locked in a 20–20 tie with the Tampa Bay Buccaneers. It was the first week of the 2002 season. With just three minutes left in overtime, Tampa Bay faced a fourth and long. They were deep in their own end.

Punter Tom Tupa stood in the back of the end zone. As Tupa took the snap, Saints special teams player Fred McAfee burst up the middle. To avoid McAfee, Tupa kept the ball and tried to escape. As McAfee was about to sack him, Tupa threw the ball up in the air.

Saints rookie James Allen caught the pass in the end zone. It was Allen's first and only career interception and touchdown. It is also the only pick-six ever thrown by a punter in league history.

Tupa earned another spot in the history books. He is the first player in the NFL to score a two-point conversion. Tupa ran the ball in on a fake extra point attempt in 1994.

Bucs punter Tom Tupa also played quarterback in college and the NFL, but he didn't look like a natural passer on this fateful play.

# CHAPTER 3

# RUNAWAY RUNS

## COMEBACK KINGS

Of the New England Patriots' six Super Bowl wins, none was more unlikely than Super Bowl LI. Though favored, the Pats fell behind the Atlanta Falcons. It was 28–3 late in the third quarter. No team in Super Bowl history had come back to win after trailing by so much.

The Falcons had played great, and the Patriots had played poorly up until that point. But they were a powerful team. The Patriots were not quitters. New England began its comeback. Its offense and defense came alive. Running back James White led the way with two touchdowns and a two-point conversion. With less than a minute remaining, the Patriots tied the score at 28. The game went into overtime.

James White scored the winning touchdown and broke Super Bowl records for most receptions (14) and points scored (20). But Tom Brady won the Super Bowl MVP. He completed 43 of 62 passes for 466 passing yards, also Super Bowl records. It was Brady's fourth Super Bowl MVP award.

In overtime, quarterback Tom Brady and the Patriots took the opening kickoff and drove 73 yards to the Atlanta two-yard line. On second and goal, Brady called White's number. The running back took the pitch and swept to the right, diving for the end zone. The nose of the ball crossed the goal line just before his knee hit. The Patriots had done it. They were Super Bowl champions again!

James White had to break several tackles to reach the end zone for a TD.

# RUNNING FOR THE RECORD BOOK

Former Falcons quarterback Michael Vick rushed for more than 6,000 yards in his NFL career. In 2002, Vick recorded the most rushing yards by a QB in a single game. He scorched the Vikings for 173 yards. In a back-and-forth game, Vick saved his best run for last.

The game was tied at 24 in overtime. The Falcons advanced the ball into Vikings territory. Vick lined up on second and eight from the 46-yard line. He called a **play-action** pass.

After faking the handoff, Vick rolled left. He saw open field ahead. He took off. Vick was too fast and shifty for the Vikings defenders. He weaved 46 yards through the defense and scored the winning touchdown.

Vick's single-game QB rushing record was broken in 2013. San Francisco's Colin Kaepernick rushed for 181 yards in a playoff game. It helped San Francisco beat the Green Bay Packers.

Michael Vick stunned Vikings fans with a dazzling run to the end zone in overtime.

# RECORD RUN

The San Francisco 49ers were hosting the New York Jets for the 1998 home opener. The two teams were locked in a 30–30 tie. It was overtime. The 49ers were pinned deep. They were at their own four-yard line. San Fran head coach Steve Mariucci called a **trap play**. The inside run was meant to gain short yardage. That way their punter wouldn't be punting out of the back of the end zone if they couldn't get a first down.

49ers running back Garrison Hearst had other ideas. He took the inside handoff. He bounced the run outside. A Jets defender closed in for the tackle. Hearst dropped him with a stiff-arm. Near midfield, Jets lineman Anthony Pleasant was in position to make the tackle. Hearst shook him off. It was off to the races. The 96-yard game-winning run was the longest run in 49ers history.

Garrison Hearst ran
96 yards for a TD
to defeat the Jets.

# RUNNING INTO THE
# RECORD BOOKS

Marcus Allen leads all NFL running backs with
the most career game-winning touchdowns
with 10. Jim Taylor comes in second with eight.
LaDainian Tomlinson is third with seven.

# ICE BOWL PLUNGE

The 1967 NFL Championship Game was famous for the weather. The temperature at game time in Green Bay was 13 degrees below zero. The **windchill** was nearly 50 degrees below zero. It was the coldest game in NFL history.

Bart Starr on the frozen turf at Lambeau Field during a historic 1967 NFL Championship Game

Trailing the rival Dallas Cowboys 17–14 late in the game, the Green Bay Packers advanced the ball. They made it down to the Dallas one-yard line. They tried two running plays. Dallas stopped them. Quarterback Bart Starr called time-out. It was the Packers' final time-out. Just 16 seconds remained.

The Packers could attempt an easy field goal. This would send the game into overtime. Everyone was freezing. Starr and his coach, Vince Lombardi, didn't want to play for overtime. They wanted to get out of the cold. They decided to gamble and go for the win.

Starr returned to the huddle. The teams lined up. The Packers were in formation for what looked like a handoff to Packers halfback Chuck Mercein. But as soon as the ball was snapped, Starr plunged forward. It was a QB keeper. Starr crossed the goal line. Moments later the Packers had a 21–17 victory. Starr's game-winning sneak is still seen as one of the gutsiest plays in NFL history.

# CHAPTER 4

# KINGS OF KICKING

## RECORD-SETTING BOOT

Tom Dempsey was born with no toes on his right foot. That didn't stop him from becoming a kicker in the NFL. He kicked for five teams during his 11-year NFL career. But Dempsey will forever be known for his time with the New Orleans Saints.

On November 8, 1970, Dempsey made history. The Saints were hosting the Detroit Lions. With two seconds left in the game, the Saints trailed 17–16. They brought out their kicker.

Dempsey lined up for a 63-yard field goal attempt. The NFL record was 56 yards. Dempsey was wearing his custom cleat with the squared-off toe. The ball was snapped. Dempsey took three steps. He drilled the kick. The home crowd exploded as the ball sailed through the uprights. Dempsey's kick gave the Saints the win!

Dempsey's record stood for 33 years. Broncos kicker Matt Prater kicked a 64-yard field goal against the Tennessee Titans in 2013.

# CUSTOM CLEAT

Tom Dempsey's record-setting kick was **controversial**. Some players and coaches thought his special cleat gave him an advantage. Some even accused Dempsey of putting a steel plate in the shoe. In reality the shoe was made from the same materials as a regular football cleat. It was just shaped to match Dempsey's foot. Still, in response to the complaints, the NFL banned **modified** kicking shoes in 1977.

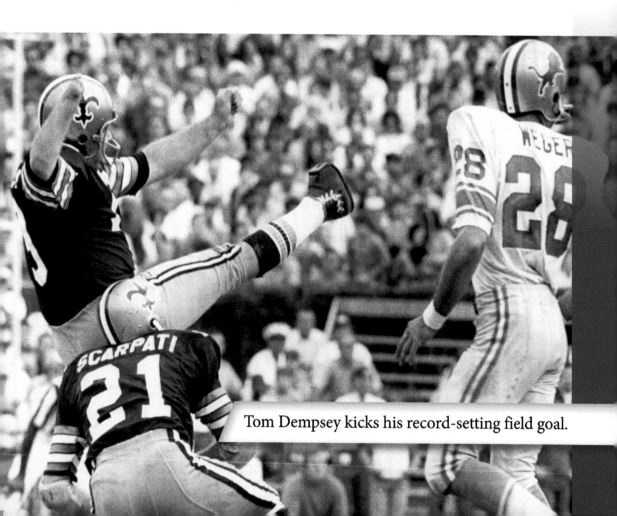

Tom Dempsey kicks his record-setting field goal.

# THE COMEBACK

The defending AFC Champion Buffalo Bills hosted the Houston Oilers for a 1992 wildcard playoff game. By halftime, the game was a blowout. Houston led 28–3.

The Oilers returned an interception for a touchdown early in the third quarter. That extended the lead to 35–3. Buffalo fans began to head for the exits. The Bills, led by backup quarterback Frank Reich, seemed totally outmatched. Then, **momentum** changed.

The Bills offense scored four touchdowns in the third quarter. The gap had closed to 35–31. Fans who remained were on their feet. They were witnessing history. The Bills tied the game at 38. The game went into overtime. It would be up to Bills kicker Steve Christie to complete the comeback. Christie lined up a 32-yard field goal in overtime. He drilled it through the uprights. The Buffalo Bills had pulled off the biggest comeback in NFL history!

Quarterback Frank Reich (14) celebrated with kicker Steve Christie as the Bills completed a record-setting comeback.

# PANTHER POWER

Over the years, a few kickers have matched or bettered Tom Dempsey's record 63-yard field goal set in 1970. Denver's Matt Prater set the new record of 64 yards in 2013. But 63 yards had been Dempsey's record alone for nearly 30 years. It was a number etched in many kickers' minds. Graham Gano, a native of Scotland, had a chance to join the club in 2018.

The Carolina Panthers trailed the New York Giants by one point. There were six seconds on the clock. Gano trotted out to line up a 63-yard attempt. The longest field goal of his career was 59 yards.

Gano knew the longer kick had a greater chance of being blocked. He had to boot the ball high enough to get it over the defensive line. But he also needed enough distance to get it there. As Gano's kick cleared the line, it looked good. As it headed toward the goalposts, it faded right. Both teams waited and watched. The kick slipped just inside the right upright. The Panthers won the game 33–31. Gano had done it.

# LONG-DISTANCE KICKS

To date, seven players have made a field goal of 63 yards or longer in an NFL game. Not all of them were game-winners, but all of them were big-time kicks.

| | PLAYER/TEAM | YEAR | DISTANCE |
|---|---|---|---|
| 1 | Matt Prater, Broncos | 2013 | 64 Yards |
| 2 | Tom Dempsey, Saints | 1970 | 63 Yards |
| 3 | Jason Elam, Broncos | 1998 | 63 Yards |
| 4 | Sebastian Janikowski, Raiders | 2011 | 63 Yards |
| 5 | David Akers, 49ers | 2012 | 63 Yards |
| 6 | Graham Gano, Panthers | 2018 | 63 Yards |
| 7 | Brett Maher, Cowboys | 2019 | 63 Yards |

Graham Gano steps into his game-winning kick.

# ICY VICTORY

In 2012 the New York Jets were on the road against the Miami Dolphins. Jets kicker Nick Folk was lined up for the game-winning field goal. The score was tied, 20–20. The ball was snapped. Folk stepped up and kicked. Dolphins defensive end Randy Starks got a hand up and blocked the potential game-winning kick. The Dolphins were still alive!

But wait.

The referees said Dolphins coach Joe Philbin had called a time-out just before the kick. Philbin was trying to "ice" Folk.

Icing the kicker is a strategy to break the kicker's rhythm by stopping play right before he kicks. There is a lot of debate about how well that works. Many kickers have said they like to get iced. It gives them time to calm down, or even get a practice kick in.

In this case, Folk made the adjustment after being iced. When the teams lined up again, he booted the game winner! Philbin's icing strategy cost the Dolphins the game.

The Dolphins' head coach tried to rattle kicker Nick Folk, but he booted a game-winner.

# CHAPTER 5

# BEST OF THE REST

## HELMET HERO

The New York Giants were taking on the undefeated New England Patriots in Super Bowl XLII. The Giants trailed 14–10 late in the fourth quarter. Eli Manning had one last drive to try to lead his team to victory.

With 1:15 left in the game, Manning faced third and five. With the snap, the Patriots came after Manning. Three Patriots surrounded the Giants QB for the sack. Somehow Manning escaped. He rolled out and threw a pass downfield. Giants receiver David Tyree was open. He leaped high in the air and grabbed the ball. Patriots cornerback Rodney Harrison tried to bat it away. Amazingly, Tyree pinned the ball to his helmet with one hand for the catch.

After his helmet catch, David Tyree never caught another pass in the NFL. His Super Bowl helmet, though, is displayed in the Pro Football Hall of Fame in Canton, Ohio.

Four plays later Manning passed to Plaxico Burress in the corner of the end zone for the game-winning touchdown. The Giants had pulled off perhaps the biggest upset in Super Bowl history.

Backup receiver David Tyree makes one of the greatest catches in Super Bowl history.

# TEBOWMANIA

Tim Tebow was a legend in college. At the University of Florida, he won the Heisman Trophy, given to the top college player. He won two national championships. Tebow was then drafted by the Denver Broncos. But playing in the pros is tough.

Halfway through the 2011 season, his second as a pro, Tebow began to shine. The Broncos were good and Tebow had led a number of fourth-quarter comebacks. He and the Broncos made the playoffs with an 8–8 record. In the wildcard round, the Broncos hosted the Pittsburgh Steelers. The favored Steelers were 12–4.

Tim Tebow fires a pass to Demaryius Thomas.

Tebow and the Broncos played well. The game went into overtime. With the game tied at 23, the Broncos won the coin toss. They would receive the kickoff. On the second play of overtime, the Broncos passed. Tebow dropped back and threw a 20-yard slant to receiver Demaryius Thomas. Thomas caught the ball in stride. He outraced the Steelers defenders 60 yards for the game-winning touchdown. Tebowmania was running wild!

Thomas heads for the end zone in a stunning playoff win.

## THE TALENTS OF TEBOW

Despite Tebow's 2011 success in Denver, he soon fell out of favor with coaches. His throwing motion was different. Some experts called it poor. He was a fine runner—but reckless. Tebow's stats were weak. He threw costly interceptions. He had a fumbling problem. After only three years playing in the NFL, Tebow was out of the league. Tebow turned to baseball. In 2016 he signed a minor league contract with the New York Mets.

# MUSIC CITY MIRACLE

A 1999 wildcard playoff game matched the Buffalo Bills against the Tennessee Titans. The Titans led 15–13 with less than two minutes to play. Bills QB Rob Johnson led his team downfield. Steve Christie kicked a field goal with 16 seconds on the clock. The Bills took the lead, 16–15.

All Buffalo had to do was shut down the Titans on the kickoff, and the game would be over. The Titans' Lorenzo Neal fielded the kickoff at the 25-yard line. Neal handed the ball to tight end Frank Wycheck. Wycheck ran to the right. He turned and threw a long **lateral** back across the field. Wide receiver Kevin Dyson caught it. With blockers in front, Dyson picked up yards. He ran untouched 75 yards for the game-winning touchdown.

Twenty years later, fans in Buffalo believe the lateral was an illegal forward pass. In Tennessee, they see it as the Music City Miracle.

On a kickoff return, Kevin Dyson received a lateral pass from a teammate and completed a long runback.

NFL Films hired a computer analyst to re-create the play and decide if Wycheck's pass was illegal. It was found to be a legal lateral pass.

# THE IMMACULATE RECEPTION

The Pittsburgh Steelers hosted the Oakland Raiders in a 1972 playoff game. It was a very physical game between two big, strong defenses. With 22 seconds left, the Steelers trailed Oakland, 7–6.

The Steelers faced a fourth-and-ten on their own 40-yard line. With no time-outs left, it was time for one last shot. Quarterback Terry Bradshaw dropped back to pass. He saw fullback John Fuqua downfield. He fired a pass. Raiders safety Jack Tatum smacked Fuqua just as the ball arrived. The ball bounced backward. But just before it hit the turf, Steelers running back Franco Harris made an amazing catch. Harris sprinted to a game-winning touchdown! The play was soon dubbed "The Immaculate Reception."

## PUNT RETURN PERFECTION

On December 19, 2010, the Philadelphia Eagles traveled to play the Giants. With 14 seconds left, the score tied at 31, New York punted. DeSean Jackson fumbled the punt at the 35-yard line. Then he picked it up and ran it back 65 yards for the touchdown! It is the only time in NFL history a game has ended with a punt return touchdown.

Franco Harris wasn't the intended receiver of Terry Bradshaw's pass, but Harris plucked it from the air after a defender tried to break up the play.

# WALK-OFF WINS

What are the biggest walk-off wins of each decade? That's a tough call, but here is a ranking for the last 60 years:

- ▶ 1960s: Bart Starr's QB keeper leads the Packers over the Cowboys in the "Ice Bowl" (1967)

- ▶ 1970s: Roger Staubach's Hail Mary pass to Drew Pearson gives the Cowboys a playoff win over the Vikings (1975)

- ▶ 1980s: 49ers quarterback Joe Montana throws a touchdown pass to Dwight Clark, whose leaping catch defeats the Cowboys in the playoffs (1982)

- ▶ 1990s: The Music City Miracle: the Titans beat the Bills 22–16 on a last-second kick return (1999)

- ▶ 2000s: Green Bay Packer Antonio Freeman makes a circus catch in overtime to beat the rival Vikings 26–20 (2000)

- ▶ 2010s: Golden Tate of the Detroit Lions tap dances along the sideline and scores to beat the Vikings 22–16 (2016)

Not every incredible walk-off happens in the National Football League. Here are a few of the best from outside the NFL.

## CAL V. STANFORD 1982

With Stanford leading Cal 20–19 with four seconds left, Cal tossed five laterals on the kickoff trying to get to the end zone. Thinking the game was over, the marching band had come onto the field. Cal's Kevin Moen took the fifth lateral and weaved through the band for the game-winning touchdown!

## IRON BOWL WALK-OFF

Tied 28–28 with host Auburn in the 2013 Iron Bowl, Alabama set up for a game-winning 57-yard field goal. The kick was wide right, and Auburn's Chris Davis caught the missed kick. He raced up the sideline and took it 109 yards for the game-winning touchdown.

## USFL RECORD-SETTER

The United States Football League (USFL) didn't last long, but one record did. The 1984 playoff matchup between the Los Angeles Express and Michigan Panthers is the longest game in professional football history. The game lasted 93 minutes and 33 seconds. It ended when Express running back Mel Gray broke a 24-yard game-winning run in triple overtime.

## CFL CRAZY KICKS

The Montreal Alouettes attempted a game-winning field goal against Toronto in a Canadian Football League (CFL) game in 2010. Toronto kicked the missed ball out of the end zone, attempting to score one point for a return. This is a legal play in the CFL. Montreal caught the kick and kicked it back into the end zone. Toronto attempted to kick it out again, and Montreal recovered in the end zone for a touchdown.

**controversial** (kon-truh-VUR-shuhl)—causing dispute or disagreement

**Hail Mary** (HAYL MAY-ree)—a play where the quarterback throws the ball deep toward the end zone in the hope that one of the team's receivers will catch it; named after a well-known prayer

**lateral** (LAT-ur-uhl)—a sideways or backward pass to another player

**modify** (MAH-deh-fi)—to make minor changes to

**momentum** (moh-MEN-tuhm)—the strength or force gained by a series of events

**pick-six** (PICK SIX)—an interception returned for a touchdown

**play action** (PLAY AK-shun)—a passing play that begins with the quarterback faking a handoff to a running back

**sudden death** (SUHD-uhn DETH)—an overtime period that ends as soon as either team scores

**trap play** (TRAP PLAY)—a running play that involves a defender getting blocked by an offensive player who lines up on the opposite side of the center

**windchill** (WIND-CHILL)—the "feels like" temperature that results from wind speed and air temperature

# READ MORE

Hetrick, Hans. *Football's Record Breakers*. North Mankato, MN: Capstone Press, 2017.

Monson, James. *Behind the Scenes Football*. Minneapolis: Lerner Publications, 2020.

Nagelhout, Ryan. *20 Fun Facts About Football*. New York: Gareth Stevens Publishing, 2016.

# INTERNET SITES

*Football Reference*
www.pro-football-reference.com

*National Football League*
www.nfl.com

*Pro Football Hall of Fame*
www.profootballhof.com

# SOURCE NOTES

P. 14: "We want the ball ..." Cindy Boren, *Washington Post*, Jan. 12, 2020, https://www.washingtonpost.com/sports/2020/01/12/seahawks-packers-have-an-unforgettable-playoff-history-just-ask-matt-hasselbeck/ Accessed March 27, 2020.

# INDEX